WLCN

Transportati

Peter Curry

Trucks
Trains

Boats
Planes

Published by Price/Stern/Sloan Publishers, Inc.
410 North la Cienega Boulevard, Los Angeles, California 90048
Text and illustrations copyright© 1983 by Peter Curry

ISBN: 0-8431-0923-8
Printed in Hong Kong

PRICE/STERN/SLOAN
Publishers, Inc., Los Angeles
1984

Drive a motor car along the road,
round the corners and bends.
Are the traffic lights red,
for us to stop,
or green, for us to go?

Drive a bus to the busy town.
It stops many times
along the road
for the passengers to get on.

Hurry aboard the fire-engine!
We must race to put out a fire.
Make way, make way,
the fire-engine sounds out loud,
as we speed through the streets.

Chug along on a tractor,
which works hard around the farm.
It pulls the plough
in long straight lines,
up and down the fields.

Fill up a big truck
with sand to carry away.
When the truck tips up
the sand falls out,
and back we go for more.

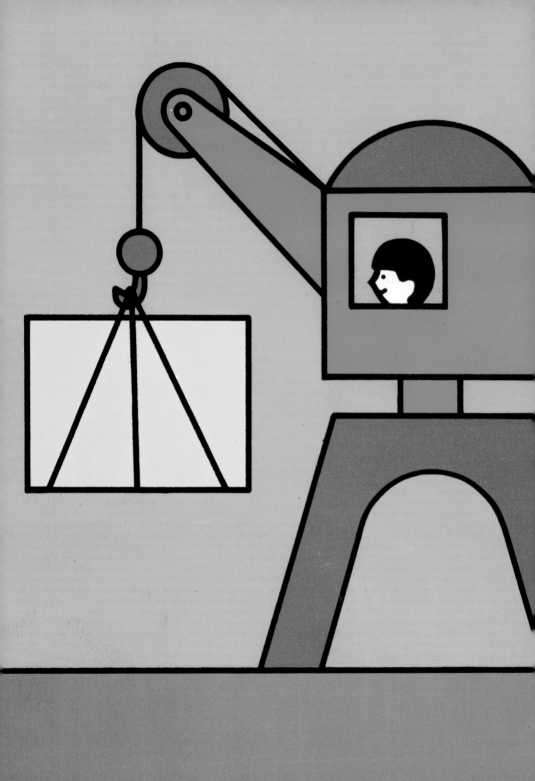

Shall we work a crane
to make it lift?
Slowly, it lifts the heavy box
up into the air.
Then it swings round
and puts the box safely down,
in just the right place.

Ride in the little cart
which the horse pulls behind.
Hear his hooves,
clip-clop, clip-clop,
as he trots along.
Gee-up, Dobbin. Gee-up.

**Dress warmly on a winter's eve
for a magical sleigh ride.
Hear the jingling bells
our reindeer wears,
as we glide across
the sparkling snow.**

Drive a steam train
which puffs along railway tracks,
pulling wagons joined on behind.
Puff-chuff, puff-chuff.
Peep-peep! blows the whistle.
Is the signal up for us to go?

Catch a fast express train
at the railway station.
We'll cross a bridge,
go through a tunnel,
and listen to the wheels
speeding down the tracks,
as everything rushes by.

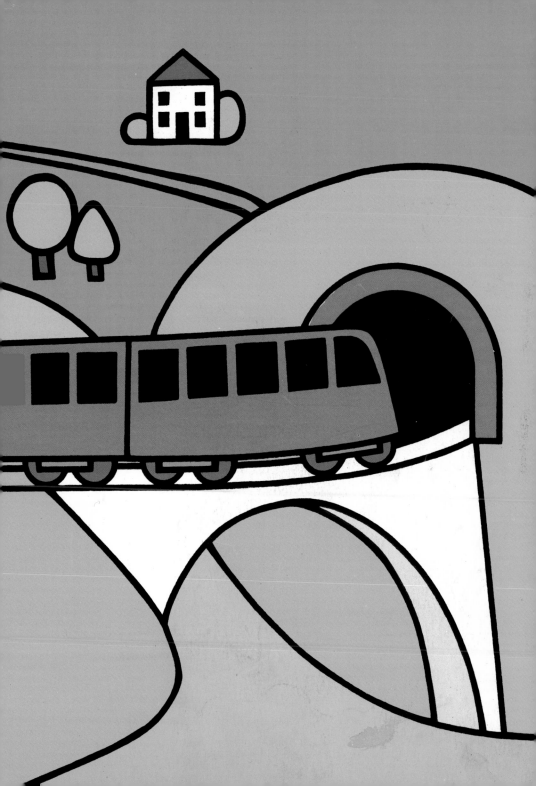

Shall we sail in a boat
upon the lake?
The wind will huff and puff
at our sails,
blowing us along
through the water.

Let's sail aboard a big ship,
upon the rolling waves.
We'll voyage across
the wide blue ocean,
to find a far-away land.

Squeeze into a submarine
and sink slowly
beneath the waves.
What shall we find, deep down,
at the bottom of the sea?

Float gently away on a giant balloon,
above roof-tops and tree-tops,
over fields and hills.
How quiet it is high up
where the birds fly.

Take off in an airplane.
Its wings will fly us high
through the clouds.
How tiny everything looks
on the ground, far down below.

Travel in a spaceship
far out into the starry sky.
Shall we go up to the moon,
and then come home, to earth?